Book One

Just
Beyond
The Sunrise

Revised Edition

By

Lorie Curry Harris

Book 1: Just Beyond The Sunset
Book 2: Colors Of Character
Lorie Curry Harris

Published By Parables
April, 2021

All Rights Reserved. No part of this book may be reproduced or utilized in any form or by any means, electronic or mechanical, including photocopying, recording, or by any information storage and retrieval system, without permission in writing from the author.

    Printed in the United States of America

Readers should be aware that Internet Web sites offered as citations and/or sources for further information may have been changed or disappeared between the time this was written and the time it is read.

Book One

Just
Beyond
The Sunrise

Revised Edition
By
Lorie Curry Harris

PUBLISHED by PARABLES
Earthly Stories with a Heavenly Meaning

Book One: Just Beyond The Sunrise

This book is dedicated to my wonderful husband Roddy. Whose love and belief in me helped me reach my dream of being a published author. He pushed me outside my comfort zone and encouraged me to just put it all out there. And to Jackie Hicks my very first fan who carries my books with her to help others. Gods blessings to all who read these pages. I pray they bring comfort.

Lorie Curry Harris

I would like to send a special thank you to my 10th grade English teacher, Mr. James Stith from Pleasure Ridge Park High School. He was the only person outside of my family at the time, I trusted to read my poetry. I presented him with every poem I had ever written and he took them home and did as I had asked. He gave me his honest opinion. He encouraged me to keep writing and pour out all my emotions into it. That is exactly what I did. His classroom was also a safe haven for me for I was bullied. Mr. Stith would notice but not point it out so as to not draw attention. Instead he would find ways to lift me up. I have never forgotten his kindness, and he deserves some credit for encouraging that 17 year old insecure girl to follow her dreams.

Table of Contents

Book One: Just Beyond The Sunrise

Autumn
The Everyday
Pray
In One's Self
Hope
Just Breathe
The Looking Glass
Restore My Soul
Crossroads
Cleansing in the Rain
Listen to the Waves
Just Be Grateful
How Can You Doubt His Existence
I Believe
Shine Brightly Your Light
Forgiveness
Pay It Forward
There Are Thorns
Unanswered Prayers
On the Outside
Passing of Time
Precious Gifts
Placed Out of Sight
Son of Her Heart
Guardian
Brothers
Carried in My Heart
No Words
How Dare You
Passer By
Dressed in Blue
The Military Wife

God and Country
Ungrateful Nation
The Silent Thief
Life's Circle
Beyond the Sunrise
No Matter How Long
Pain No One See's
Aboard
The Battle Inside
Friendship
What Is Beauty
Think Before You Speak
Song Bird
Don't See Color See Soul
Love How Is It Defined
So Long
Character
Tranquility

Autumn

All around me there seems to be
Colors of red, yellow and gold
Such beauty my eyes behold
The ever-changing scenery unfolds
Like and artist canvas
With brush strokes bold
The hillsides bursting with a palate of colors
In all of autumns wonders
As a crisp cool breeze begins to flow
The leaves descend and begin to blow
Cascading down to the ground
In a dance of reds, yellow and golds
Another season scene begins
As another ends
Like our troubles in life
Last just for a season
Remember with God
There is always a reason
 So, Like the changing autumn leaves
Let God color the seasons of your soul
And make your heart as pure as gold.

Lorie Curry Harris

The Everyday

Why does it seem
Families now a days
Only come together at funerals or holidays
What happened to the everyday
Where do our family ties lie
They are becoming tethered and torn
Lost among the hustle of everyday life
Too busy we say for a visit
No time can be made
For a talk over coffee or tea
I just can't fit you in
Oh how sad it really is
Family is our family
No matter what the calendar reads
Whether it be Christmas or New Year's Eve
No reason should ever cross our lips for no time for family
That excuse just shouldn't exist
One day in the blink of an eye it will seem
That family member will no longer be
Too late for a visit, too late to talk
Your excuses now become regret
And now your heart is burdened with what if
So please do not wait till time runs out
Make your priority to be
Time for family in every day.

Lorie Curry Harris

Pray

I pray for peace your soul will find
I pray for comfort in your heart divine
I pray for understanding in your mind
To know that all things work out in God's time
When you feel weary with everyday life
When your stressed and troubled from all the strife
You feel there is no end in sight
I pray that you look to the heavens above
And find yourself leaning on God's love
He can take away from you all the worry
The doubts, the fears that keep you up at night
The shame from your past for the mistakes that you have made
All you need do is to trust and have faith
And he will send to you all these things that I pray
For you dear friend, I ask them all
In Jesus sweet name.

Lorie Curry Harris

In One's Self

She is passionate and strong
Independent and determined
There is nothing that can bring her down
When the doctor said
I am afraid you have cancer
She made her mind up then and there
This would not defeat her
Her strong will and love for life
Kept her going through this tremendous fight
As the chemicals coursed through her veins
Attacking this toxic invader
Sickness is robbing her of her health
Her body is plagued with disease
She is tired her flesh is weak
And she is sick of being sick
But even still this does not break her spirit
For in her heart, she knows
There is not situation so desperate
No diagnosis so grim
That will deter her from trusting
That hope is never lost faith is never far
If in yourself you will always believe.

Lorie Curry Harris

Hope

Hope is such a simple word
But for those who believe
It holds the most meaning
When things in your life seem out of control
When back where turned from friends you have known
When all you believe you begin to doubt
When those you have trusted break your heart
And you begin to feel there is no way out
As the weight of the world is on your shoulders
At least for you it seems that way
When nothing seems to be going right
Sleep cannot claim you
As you toss and turn at night
When you want to quit
Throw your hands in the air
Scream to the wind I am done
Life deals you disappointments
People will let you down
And stress can overwhelm you
But there is nothing you can't overcome
At this moment remember
Nothing is hopeless
Just find your strength and believe.

Lorie Curry Harris

Just Breathe

Just breathe, not just the air to fill your lungs
But to breathe life in, it has just begun
Cherish each moment, each stepping stone
Don't take for granted what tomorrow holds
Take a moment to stop and pause
Listen to the birds sing their song
Flying through the air dancing along
Just breathe in the scent of the day
The fragrant smell after the rain
Do not stress over the corporate race
Or fuss over deadlines not made
Just breathe, take your time
Don't rush through your days
Till your life is gone
No need to figure out tomorrow today
Just breathe, don't take life so seriously
All things will work together
For those who believe
So just breathe and wait and see
What your life unfolds to be.

Lorie Curry Harris

The Looking Glass

Peering in the looking glass
What reflection do you see
Who is that there before you
The person that you see
Do you notice the lines upon your face
Each one tells a story, of time and place
The road you have traveled
The decisions you have made
All read like a book written on a page
Are you strong and independent
From the battles that you've faced
Or bitter and hard hearted
Are you forgiving and sincere
Towards those who've done you wrong
Or cold and indifferent
From the pain they have caused
Do you have faith and remain steadfast
When trials and valleys you must face
Or shake your fist to the heavens
And ask of God why
When seeing others struggle
Do you find empathy for them
Try to help or offer a prayer
Or do you shrug your shoulders
And say why should I care
People come into our lives for a reason
Even if just for a short while
Obstacles are set in our path
To make us stronger and continue to grow
To build our strength and character to show

Lorie Curry Harris

Our inner soul to the world
So they can all know
Through it all God is faithful and true
So when peering into the looking glass
Is this what others will see in you
Does this define what your reflection shows
Tis something only you can know.

Restore My Soul

Restore my soul
Oh Lord I pray
Help me find strength to face each day
At times I feel so all alone
As darkness crosses over my soul
And my heart cries
As a sadness fills my entire being
For reasons I do not know
I cannot answer why
My life is full, I'm fulfilling my dreams
But my soul is empty somethings missing
Then it occurs to me
As I watch the birds outside sing
And see the tree limbs blow in the breeze
I hear a whisper in the wind
Remember me, do you miss me
It's you Lord, I've left you behind
I've become so busy with everyday task
The hustle and bustle of life's demands
That even when the night time comes
And at last, I lay my head to rest
Even now at the close of the day
I can't even find time to pray
Shame over comes me
And conviction strikes my heart
How can my soul find joy
My life find purpose
If I leave my savior out
I fall to my knees that instant
And beg for his forgiveness

Lorie Curry Harris

At that very moment
The darkness fades
My heart is full
And my soul has been restored
With the peace and comfort and eternal joy
That can only be found in God's great graces.

Crossroads

You've come to a crossroads
Your fork in the road
Time to decide which way you will go
Do you stick with the familiar?
Or brave the unknown
Find your courage to move forward
But first you must learn to let go
Face the demons of your past
Deal with the struggles that were set in your path
Do you allow yourself to grow bitter?
For the mistakes you've made the trials you have faced
Or instead, be grateful thankful to God
For bringing you through and molding you
Into the strong empathetic person, you have now become
A person of character and strength
Compassion and forgiveness
For you know that's exactly what God shown to you
Now your life can be a testament to him
For where your life is now and where you have been
So, choose your path wisely
Which way will you go?
Stay on the familiar the path of the past
Or give it all over to God
And trust solely on him
The road won't always be easy
But rest assured
For God is the only one
Who has your best interest at heart
His plans for your life

Are greater than yours
With God at the head
You can be so much more
It's your crossroads
Which way will you go?
It's all up to you
God is waiting to know.

Cleansing in The Rain

Your soul lay marked with scars
Your heart is broken in two
The person you were before is no more
You find it difficult to face each day
For your storms seem endless
You have lost your way
The dark clouds that loom before you
Are only results of your doubt
For your self-worth lies in the rumble
From all the storm has destroyed
The wind that whispers feeds your storm
As the words wash away your dignity
But it's time to let go and move forward
So, let the rain wash over your soul
Poor down upon you till all doubt is no more
For God gave the promise of the rainbow, after the storm
For there is cleansing in the rain
To bring to the surface all doubt and fear
To make what God has envisioned us to be
So, embrace your storm
Dance in the rain
Let it wash away all things from before
Stand proudly and boldly
For facing your storms
For letting go and letting God
Yes, my friends
There is cleansing in the rain.

Lorie Curry Harris

Listen To The Waves

Walking along the shore line
With the wet sand between my toes
My eyes take in the grander
Of the scene that there unfolds
The ocean waves now call my name
If you listen for you, they do the same
The white wave caps rolling in
Back and forth back and forth
Can you feel yourself begin to sway?
Listen to the rhythm in the waves
See the sunlight dancing like birds in flight
Upon the top of the water
Trickery of movement and light
A symphony of sensory
Is what your eyes delight
Watch the tide wash over the shore line
Brushing the sand ever so briefly
With the gentlest touch
Then it moves back out to sea
If you sit very still
And close your eyes to hear
You can hear the rhythm in the waves
The song that's being played
The symbolism that can be found
Upon the ocean tide
Listen now with your heart
And you will surely find
The back and forth of the waves
The way you begin to sway
It's God our father rocking you

The sunlight dancing on the waves
Are the joys in your life
When his light shown down on you
The tide washing over the shore line
Is like his blood washing over you
Carrying all the things from before
Out to sea
Where they will be remembered no more
The waves crashing in turning about
With their white caps
Are the trials you have faced in your life
But there will be a calming of the sea
With the gentlest touch
You hear in the breeze be still
You listen to the symphony
There is reason in the ocean waves.

Just Be Grateful

As our lives take twist and turns
We experience happiness, joy and tragedy
But often we focus only on the hurts
When times in our lives become darkest
And we forget the sunny joyful days
It's at those times you need just to be grateful
We weren't promised only sunny skies
The rain and storms will come
But it's in the dark days as we weather the storm
That we are taught to be grateful
Because it is when we learn God's grace
He carries us through in his loving embrace
But it's not without us doing our part
For there are lessons to be learned
Forgiveness to be given
And empathy for others to be felt
When in the storms you find yourself
So instead of saying why me
Look to the heavens and be grateful
For God is molding you into the person
Who he believes you to be
So just be grateful.

Lorie Curry Harris

How Can You Doubt His Existence?

You see the mountain peaks standing tall
And yet you doubt he exist at all
You see the ocean blue
And yet you doubt his word is true
You see the trees move in the breeze
And yet you doubt his victories
You feel the coldness of winter
And yet your heart remains bitter
You see the wondrous of spring
And maybe in your heart you now believe
As you witness all of nature's beauty
How can you doubt when it all began
With just the touch of God's mighty hand.

Lorie Curry Harris

I Believe

I believe in the power of prayer
When bowed down on bended knee
God hears our cares
I believe he sends healing to those who are sick
Whether it be in body or heart
Our needs are met
I believe for those sincere
Our souls are saved
Our sins are washed away
I believe we can go astray
Make mistakes
Take the wrong pathway
But I also believe
God forgives and forgets
Though we never may
I believe a second chance
He will always give
To those who are his
Yes, I believe in saving grace
I believe in his healing touch
I believe his mercy is astounding
I believe through faith
I believe, I believe, I believe
Because my friend
He did this all in me
And he can also do this for thee.

Lorie Curry Harris

Shine Brightly Your Light

Sometimes it seems
Your life is like
A candle burning bright
Flickering in the wind
You fear at any moment
The slightest gust
Will steal your candles light
You tend to it
With the greatest of care
Safe keeping away
The shadows lingering there
For they play out your life's story
With the flickering of the light
The dancing shadows on the wall
Tell your story to all
But that's what made you who you are
The flickering stories on the wall
So, embrace what's made you who you are
And remember your candles light
Burns from your soul
No need to tend
What God has made whole.

Lorie Curry Harris

Forgiveness

Forgiveness such a simple word
But so hard to give
Those who have wronged us in our lives
Caused so much strife
We withhold forgiveness from those
Feel we are justified or given the right
To hold a grudge to those for life
After all they were the ones in the wrong
Really..is that what you believe to be right
To harbor bitterness in your heart
You hurt only yourself
Even damage your health
When from others forgiveness you withhold
How is it you can't ask of yourself
What you ask God to do
Then who are we
To ask God to forgive.

Lorie Curry Harris

Pay It Forward

Remember the philosophy to
Pay it forward
A kindness done for you
Just pay it forward
What a chain reaction that would make
Each continuing to do for another
But this day and age
No one has time except for oneself
To busy text messaging to even notice to see
The homeless family on the street
How much time out of your day
Would it take
To give them some food or a blanket or two
That may be the compassion they need
To finally get off the streets
And pay it forward to a person they meet
While shopping the stores
You don't notice the girl
Sticking items in her coat
Maybe if you took a moment to hear
The story of why she is shop lifting here
Give the resources to care for herself
And no longer have the need to steal
She then pays it forward to someone she meets
Oh, what a world this surely would be
If we could just pay it forward
To those in need
You never know the people you meet
What a difference you made
By the kind jester you gave

Isn't that simply what God ask of us
Offer compassion, help for those in need
Seriously how hard can it be
Just pay it forward
It's simple really
You'll never know what a difference you made.

There Are Thorns

We were not promised an easy road
That our lives would be free of valleys deep
Or that those we love would not have to leave
No promise made of not facing tribulations
For hard times we would surely see
We will know pain
Betrayal and doubt
Heartache and loss
For life always comes at a cost
We are given free will at birth
Which way will you choose
What life will you lead
Will always be your testimony
Did you hold to your faith
Sometimes we stumble and fall
Trust in God and believe
Your stronger for your struggles
For even with the beauty of the rose
There are thorns.

Lorie Curry Harris

Unanswered Prayers

You bow your head
While on bended knee
Cry out to God what it is that you need
No time is taken to ponder and wait
No patience our heavenly Father thinks
The answer you seek
Take time to reveal
Whether it's mending of heart
Or healing the ill
Maybe it's indecision or fear
You have questions about
No need to distrust
Just be still and wait
God works all things out
But to your dismay
It may not happen in the way
You wanted God to answer
If you feel he answered at all
Maybe the mending to you took too long
Or the healing you sought took your loved one home
Your indecision and fear
Simply takes faith on your part
For God as you know
Has your best interest at heart
For all prayers are answered
Even if for you it appears..unanswered.

Lorie Curry Harris

On The Outside

She sees him there in his home
With his children and grandchildren gathered near
She feels she is on the outside looking in
At these people familiar yet unknown
Inside this home warmth is found
Inside their hearts love abounds
He has lived a life she doesn't know
She listens intently as stories are told
For her memory is short from the things long ago
He catches her eye and for a moment she tries
To look deep enough inside to find
The man she once knew and longs to know again
He smiles that smile she remembers still
That made her laugh and knew all is well
He is there now for each milestone of her life
Every birthday, every dream fulfilled
Each accomplishment she has reached
To let her know she can count on him
He will never leave again, for daddy's don't leave
Maybe one day she will begin to feel
She is not on the outside looking in
And she will know the man she calls dad.

Lorie Curry Harris

Passing of Time

As a child you danced upon his feet
You giggled and laughed as he twirled you about
When night time came and you drifted to sleep
In his strong arms he carried you to bed
And tucked you tightly in
As the years went by
He taught you how to drive
His patience was astonishing
And when that big day came
He walked you down the aisle
With tears in his eyes and gave you away
Through the years you've turned to him
For guidance and advice
But now it seems
His steps are slower
His reactions not as quick
There is a cloudiness that covers his thoughts
A dimness to his sight
His age is showing, that is undeniable
Now a hand he needs with help to bed
Or a walk across the floor
My fear is a day soon approaching
When he will no longer be
Father of time is stealing away
The father of mine.

Lorie Curry Harris

Precious Gifts

Crayon marks juice box treats
Tiny little running feet
Laughter in the air like song birds sing
Building blocks, dolls and trikes
Works of art on the ice box
Hugs and kisses and joy abounds
Inside a house where love is found
What a precious gift from above
You have been bestowed
To share your life with a child
And watch them grow
The days and years to come
Will be bitter sweet
For a time will come when they will leave
Live their own life and raise a family
One day for you will come
When you stand before the one
Who gave to you this precious gift
Will you say to him with a shrug of shoulders
I done my best
Or reply this way
I raised them with patience, kindness and love
I disciplined and showed right from wrong
I taught them of your love and grace
For I knew one day you I would face
And stand in judgement for the trust you placed
In me to raise a child of faith
This precious gift I did not take for granted
I lived my life before them by example
So, they would know of your love and grace

On your judgement day
When before him you stand face to face
Will you say I done my best
Or will you reply
I lived a life of faith
Will your children testify to the same?
Or will you hang your head in shame
Don't take your gifts for granted
For one day you will have to answer
For the precious child you've been given.

Placed Out Of Sight

You will find her there
In her rocking chair
Humming a familiar tune
Her room is small
Her memories in frames upon the wall
Her body defeats her
For it has become frail
But who she is, what defines her
Is all still there
Silent tears stroll down her cheeks
As her life plays out in her mind
The nurses and staff all know her stories
For they have become friends
She fell in love in her early youth
Raised a family
Nurtured and loved them
Giving them the best of her
They grew up and raised a family of their own
And she became grandma
How delighted she was in this roll
Encircling them all in love
Then later in life she became a widow
Her knowing such great sorrow
But comfort she still gave
To her children and grandchildren
Now elderly in years
They all have place her here
Out of sight in this home
Too busy for a phone call
No time to visit the mother, the grandmother

Who gave to them her all
So, her eyes wonder
To the pictures on the wall
She thinks to herself
Will they ever visit or call?
The nurse standing outside her room in the hall
Sends up a silent prayer
Dear God please let her children
Give to this woman
At least a little of what she has given them
Before she becomes
Just a memory on the wall.

Son Of Her Heart

Although you were not a child of her womb
She claims you as her own
Your second mom, your home away from home
This selfless woman who gave to you
Your hiding place, your safe refuge
You could always find in her a warm embrace
A comforting tone and humble grace
An encouraging word to lift you up
So you could reach all you have ever dreamed
Her understanding eyes told to you
There is nothing you can't achieve
She inspired in you to always believe
No matter what you face
She will be your protector, your friend
And your biggest fan
Her gentle motherly ways
Has turned you into the man you are today
You the son of her heart
And she your Momma Hart.

Lorie Curry Harris

Guardian

What honor has been bestowed
As you watch and partake
This little one grow
It has been entrusted to you
To instill values and responsibility
Upon this little one's soul
You are to help guide and protect
To love and make time to share
Your life with this child
For you take seriously your role
For another to think so highly of you
To give you this honor
Of being guardian
One day you know
You will take pride in the thought
Though they were not part of you
They will always know
You loved them as your own
For that was simply your role…guardian.

Lorie Curry Harris

Brothers

As children they pulled your pigtails
Put salt in your sweet tea
Teased you until you screamed
"I'm telling mom!"
As their little sister
You always wanted to tag along
But then they started to say
"No girls allowed"
But yet, whenever you would fall down
They stop right away and pick you up
In their tender young voices
Ask if you were alright
In the teenage years, a lot of things changed
The bikes were put away
And cars now filled the driveway
Hugs were out grown
They now simply say
"Hey sis, how was your day?"
We now fought over the phone
For it continually rang
But when a young man would come to the door
They would say "You have to go through me"
A smile spreads across my face to think about those days
My brothers the protectors always there for me
Now as adults it's huge hugs
And I love you sis
I think brothers are guardian angles
Sent from above.

Lorie Curry Harris

Carried In My Heart

I went to visit you today
Updated you about my life
Told you of goals reached and dreams achieved
Then a smile came across my face
As memories flooded my mind
Just as quickly as they came
A sadness swept my heart
For I wonder if you hear me
Do you know I visit you?
A stone that bares your name
Speaks not a word
As tears stream down my face
A soft wind sweeps through
And in that moment, I know it's you
Though your voice I do not hear
Though your face I do not see
You're the guardian angel looking over me
One day we will meet again
But until then
I know that you are near
For your always carried with me
In my heart.

Lorie Curry Harris

No Words

There are no words
For times like these
When those we love, have to leave
Words of comfort go unheard
As sorrow sweeps over our souls
We feel alone in a crowd of mourners
Stricken with the knowledge to know
The void that we will forever feel
For a piece of our heart is buried with those
That we called loved ones and friends
But a day will come
When you will smile again
As you treasure the memories of those
Who lay silent in the grave
Comfort will encompass your whole being
Because we know one day
When the Lord calls us home
You will see your loved one once again.

Lorie Curry Harris

How Dare You

How dare you
How could you do such a thing
Leave your family and friends to grieve
How selfish an act
How thoughtless could you be
Impose upon us this cruelty
Leave us here with all these questions and doubt
Bury our loved one who seemed to believe
This was the only way out
Oh, how cowardly
The effects of your actions
Will ripple through time
Being felt by all you left behind
You let the darkness take over your mind
Destroying the person you are inside
The demons won that day
The day you committed suicide
I always thought you were stronger than that
For we always knew a greater power than these
One who could overcome the darkness with ease
You had to only trust and believe
And he would have delivered you
From all of these things
A comfort and peace only he can provide
So maybe it was a gift he gave that day… compassion,
when we laid you in the grave.

Lorie Curry Harris

Passer By's

The world turned a little darker today
For your light no longer remains
The bird songs are not as sweet
The warm sunrays not as bright
Fragrant flowers no longer smell
For earthly things that here remain
Have lost some of their glory
For you have left this world for your eternal home
Leaving the rest of us to roam alone
The people passing on the street
Smiling, laughing, talking
Do not feel the loss of your passing
For your smiling face they did not meet
Your tender heart they did not know
Your warm embrace never encircled those
Of the passing people on the street
For the world continues on, never stopping
Or even taking a pause
For the precious loved one
Who has gone
But for those of us who knew you best
The days will move slower
Our pace not as quick
Our hearts will always lay heavy
From the void left by your passing
When the passers on the street
Begin to wonder
Why the sun is not so bright
The birds not singing quite as much
They may shrug their shoulders

And pass it off
But as each loved one leaves this earth
It becomes a lesser place
It's value decreasing
For our home is of another world
That some see sooner than others.

Dressed In Blue

They took an oath to protect and serve
To enforce and uphold our countries law
Be placed in harm's way when duty calls
When shots ring out in the night
Or screams being heard from a domestic fight
Drugs being sold on your neighborhood streets
Children abducted and taken from home
Crime is sweeping our nation, so we are told
But no fear you will find upon their face
Of the officers who choose to pursue
The bravery of those dressed in blue
Sacrificing themselves to protect you
So, as you stroll through the public park
Shop the malls and grocery stores
Travel the highways alone at night
Don't forget the ones who respond
When you need to dial 911.

Lorie Curry Harris

The Military Wife

She is there on the home front
Going through the routine of everyday life
Keeping up the household, paying the bills
Caring for their children
She is just going through the motions
Keeping the promise, she made
For the last words from her husband she heard
Was him saying "stand strong"
She wants so badly to make him proud
So, she puts on a brave face
Laughs and smiles with their children everyday
But at nighttime when she is all alone
Wearing his pajamas
Clinging to his pillow in bed
The tears flow freely down her face
The fear of where he is
What he is going through
And will he ever make it home again
All begins to sink in
She took a vow to love, honor and obey
He too did the same
But not only to her but to country as well
She bows her head and begins to pray
For protection over her husband
For comfort to calm her worries and fears
And for patience to help her while waiting
For the day she longs to see
To be in her husband's warm embrace
To final be standing face to face
To hear from his lips, I love you

She hopes with all she has
That their reunion day will come
That her biggest fear will not come true
That a casket she meets instead
Draped in red, white and blue
Oh, how she hopes and prays
To his face she can finally say
With worry and fear all gone
Welcome home my love, welcome home
A family they are again
Well, at least until he is deployed again.

God And Country

They close the clasp that held their helmets
Checked one last time their ammo packs
Sat silently in their landing crafts
As the sea rocked against them
They ponder the memories of home
For the battle that rages they soon will join
They must suppress their fear
As they storm upon the shore line
They went in blind no way to know
The enemy sat in waiting
Gun fire rings out at the first step made
And men begin to fall
Screams are heard, insanity is seen
At these lives lost upon the beach
Reinforcements come, but for most to late
Letters of condolences are sent to those
Left behind by these brave souls
No time to mourn
Must move on
For not even death
Stops the battle clock
This brotherhood of those
With uniforms the same
Stood for God and country
If as a nation we cannot do the same
Then we should surely
Hang our heads in shame.

Lorie Curry Harris

Ungrateful Nation

You see on the news
The celebration of a game
A sports event
Or even an Olympian
Banners are waved, cheers are heard
Parties are thrown
And even flags waved
But where was the celebration
Parties and balloons
When the war was finally declared over
And our military began to come home
No cheers were heard
Or sadly even a flag waved
What a welcome home for the brave
I wonder how they felt
When on American soil
Only to find themselves forgotten
By those they fought for
Are we that ungrateful a nation
To think so highly of a sporting even
Then we do our military
Something to surely think about.

Lorie Curry Harris

The Silent Thief

They have been married for over forty years
Neither can remember a day without the other
They met in high school becoming the best of friends
There was nothing they didn't share with one another
So, no one was surprised when he took her for his bride
Just two weeks after graduation
No one could deny the love you had seen in their eyes
No greater love had there ever been witnessed
Even their children as they grew to adults
Always knew the love their parents shared
For at times somehow it would seem
They were intruders watching a dream
Not one night did they spend apart
They finished each other's sentences with ease
But now somethings different, somethings changed
The look in her eyes at times seems confused
She forgets the simplest things
He reaches for her ever so gently
And says "I love you my darling I love you the best"
Then she smiles and says
"Until the day I'm laid to rest"
With that she settles closely in his arms
Never noticing the tears silently falling down his face
For he knows she is slipping away
Some days are good days, she remembers everything
But some days more often than not
She can't even remember his name
This silent thief that came from nowhere
Started stealing her memories away

One by one little by little
And he knows one day will come
When his precious love remembers nothing
The love they shared the family they made
The vastness of their love
He grieves each day a part of her dies
When she looks at him with vacant eyes
But for now, he will just hold her
And whisper their love vow
"I love you my darling I love you the best"
And she continues to finish the very last verse
"Until the day I'm laid to rest.

Book One: Just Beyond The Sunrise

Life's Circle

I went to the park today
People watching if you may
And there it was right before me
Life's stages from infancy
To the golden years
Some just beginning
And others journey coming to an end
Life's circle being witnessed there
In just the ordinary
What stories you could find
By simply watching expressions
Cross over their face
An elderly woman sitting there
Watching her grandchildren play
I wonder what she's thinking
Does she worry of their future?
With the way things are this day and age
Does she think of what they will become
When they are longer children at play
Or does she think instead
What for them is she leaving behind
I'm not speaking of material things
But instead of impressionable things of mind
Will they remember what she stood for
What she believed, the love she left for them
For the day she is gone
Then I watch her, as her eyes witness a young couple
The mother holding her young babe
And dad on the swings with his toddler

She then begins to chuckle
For she knows their days ahead
For them their journey is just beginning
As laughter is heard across the park
She takes in the whole scene
Babies, toddlers and families just beginning
And others farther along in their journey
With school age children with field trips
And school plays in their future
And oh yes, the teenage years she thinks
Good luck with that a battle you surely face
Then it's bitter sweet for then it's off to college
Back to herself she now reflects
As she continues to watch her grandchildren at play
A huge smile spreads across her face
For this is the way it should be
The circle of life, it's never complete
It just continues on round and round
Never ending just continuing with new beginnings.

Beyond The Sunrise

Tomorrows' sunrise will come again
Another day will come to stay
The nightingale will sing no more
With the dawning of the day
As the morning light
Creeps through your window drapes
Your awakened from your slumbered sleep
As your dreams from the night before
Begin to dissipate, a new day you must face
Though your heart is burdened from your struggle
You find your inner strength within
A courage you have discovered
From facing the vastness of your troubles
Your comfort is found in the love that abounds
From the ones that you call family
There is a smile down deep in your soul
For what you have always known
You do not face your trials alone
There is always hope
Just beyond the sunrise.

Lorie Curry Harris

Book One: Just Beyond The Sunrise

No Matter How Long

She is standing there at the podium
Amazed at the people gathered there today
Her face is wrinkled with age
Her hair is salt pepper gray
As she takes a deep breath to begins to speak
A smile spreads across her face
As memories of where she was
And what her life is now
Is still astonishing to believe
When her first words leave her mouth
She is transported back in time
To a younger form of herself
Oh, how she wishes she could tell her
All of what she knows now
But she continues with the story of her youth
For there are lessons to be learned
You see she found herself married
To a man she really never knew
Oh he was charming, a smooth talker too
But after the words I do
His demeanor changed and his darkness grew
Fear was an emotion she became accustom to
He controlled everything she did or said
Isolation there began
No family, no friends
So she would have only him
No one to tell her secrets to
No one to show the bruises she wore
His words were worse than his fist
For they cut deeper, they destroyed more

They tore her down till she was nothing
The words took away her self-worth
Her confidence her self esteem
The words stay in her mind
Till this very day
The physical abuse took her freedom away
For fear imprisoned her to refrain
From ever voicing how she thinks or feels
The combination of the two
Destroyed her spirit till she was broken
Now just sleep walking
Or so it would seem
Through her life feeling nothing
Numbness had overcome her
Till one day she had had enough
Her soul was screaming out
And in her ear she heard this whispered
"You deserve so much more, my plans for you are greater than this,
My child this is not love this is not my will for you"
With that she left the very next day
Her only possession the clothes on her back
She was scared to death
But it was a different kind of fear
Fear of the unknown and what her life holds
But no longer fear of abuse
Her journey was hard, her recovery long
But in the end, she found herself
Her soul began to sing again
Her heart learned to love
Her mind, well... will always be healing
For she still doesn't go out after dark

She still looks in her rearview mirror
And always carries her mace
Even now when darkness falls
An unsettling feeling creeps through
But she shakes it off
And focuses instead on the life she has now
And where God has led
How blessed she feels to truly be loved
To have survived her trauma
People still ask her to this day
I don't understand, why did you stay
That is why I'm here today
To tell my story so maybe you can see
It's not that easy just to leave
You believe what they tell you
You are not worth a thing
And as sad as it is, you even believe
You deserved the abuse you receive
Yes, I know that all isn't true
But I had to leave to find the truth
Even now to this very day
If my dear husband startles me in my sleep
I get scared and scream
So this is what I ask of you
Give understanding to those who were abused
Though their flesh is healed
Their mind has been counseled
Their heart has found true love
Scars still lay marked upon their soul
No matter how many years they live.

Lorie Curry Harris

Pain You Can't See

No one knows the frustration that is felt
From the pain this situation has dealt
Every day you draw a breath and steady yourself
For this and each day you must face
With each task you set out to do
Pain radiates through your whole being
You want to just scream out and cry
But instead, you keep it all inside
Every movement you make
Every step you take
No matter the simplicity
It still causes you pain
You feel so utterly alone in your daily struggle
So incredibly misunderstood
Because no one can see with their eyes
The chronic pain you feel each day
You some how feel less than you are
For the limitations you now face
The things you usc to lovc to do
Are now out of the question
Depression creeps inside your soul
And anger is felt in your heart
For your life has forever been changed
Your limitations will always remain
But tomorrow's sunrise will come again
You will find your strength within
Face each new day with a smile
For nothing happens without reason
Not for us to ask why
For God in his wisdom

Lorie Curry Harris

Will not give us more than we can bare
For all of this last for just a season.

Aboard

Excitement could be felt in the crowd that day
For history was being made
No one had ever seen
Such beauty upon the sea
No grander vessel had ever been built
As she left the dock and began her voyage
Friends and family waved from the shore line
Some set sail in search of a dream
Others for prosperity or social esteem
If in first class no expense was spared
From the grand staircase, the china plates
The formal dinners and smoking rooms
Or the elegance of their quarters
But if traveling below decks in third
Discrimination is what you felt
For you were just the working class
On a cold and dreary night
Fate revealed her secret
As the iceberg they did hit
With such a tragedy you would think
It wouldn't matter the class you traveled
But those below found gates locked shut
As water came rushing in
Just give us a chance you heard them scream
Those above were running frantic
As life boats left so quickly
No one understood why they weren't completely filled
Fear was seen on every face
As this majestic ship began to sink
Parents clinging tightly to their children

Spouses whispering their last I love you
For those who found themselves
In the freezing cold sea, they shivered in their skin
Ice cycles were forming in their hair
They were filling their lungs with the frigid air
The blackened night sky with specks of starlight
Maybe the last they ever see
What desperation, what hopelessness
For those treading water in the sea
For most this would be their final resting place
Boats that were floating near by
For those aboard
Will now have to live
With the question why
I survived and they did not
I heard their calls for help
And I answered not
Will their souls ever know peace?
This inside the minds
Aboard the ship titanic

The Battle Inside

A battle rages inside the mind
Of those hoping to find
Solace and calming from that which binds
For your life has become afflicted
With raging emotions and doubt
One day you're on this manic high
With energy to burn and happy with life
The next you feel utterly lost
Hopeless and alone
Your so confused by this chaos
No way to muddle through
Your life at seems
In such disarray, an upheaval of sorts
This emotional roller coaster ride
No way to get off
People misunderstand you
Your family is at a loss
Your anxiety builds
Your irritable and cross
You want to scream at the top of your lungs
Stop this madness inside me
This state of unrest
Is there any help please
Then there is a new day dawning
Another day to get through
Maybe it will be a good day
There is no way to know
Not with those with bipolar
Only time knows.

Lorie Curry Harris

Friendship

The word friend is used so easily
But what does it really mean?
Is a friend a coworker you talk to in passing?
No, an acquaintance this would be
Is a friend your neighbor
You talk pleasantries with
No this is just politeness
Friendship is a relationship
A connection with another
Some were made in childhood
And some later in life
A friend is a person you can count on
You can talk to and trust
A person who is there for you
No matter what
And no matter how long it may have been
Since you last saw or spoke to one another
Your connection is still there
A friend will come when you call
A friend will comfort and guide
A friend always has a listening ear
True friendship lasts a lifetime
When given the definition of friendship
Who would you truly call friend?

Lorie Curry Harris

What Is Beauty

What is beauty
Is it the features of someone's face
The color of their skin
Or the heritage of their race
These are all just superficial
Appealing to the eyes
Beauty is not something found on the outside
But instead, is found inside the soul
Whether your young and youthful or wise and old
This is where your personality abides,
On the inside
We use the word beautiful so easily
Like gorgeous and breath taking
But what is all of that really
Does a person take your breath away
Make you stop in your tracks and say
Oh wow… how beautiful
No, I don't think so
Beauty is found in a selfless act
A word spoken in kindness
Or a sacrifice made for others
A person who gives freely of themselves
Seeking nothing in return
Someone who is just doing what is right
That simple really
Yes, this is what I call beauty.

Lorie Curry Harris

Think Before You Speak

Sometimes you don't stop to think
Listen to your conscience as it speaks
You just go ahead and do
Never giving a thought
To what your actions would ensue
What words spoken in anger
Or with a sarcastic tone
Would affect the feelings of those
You say are your friends or family
What price is actually paid
For the laughter and jokes made
At another's expense
Do you think so little of yourself
That you find it necessary
To belittle others
Is the smirk you wear upon your face
Worth the price that's paid
One day you will find yourself alone
If you cannot learn
To have consideration for others
If within yourself you cannot love
So, step back and think
Before a word is ever said
For more contentment is found in kindness
More joy in a kind word spoken
Then there will ever be found
In a condescending action
So trade your smirk for a genuine smile
Because you cannot hide

Lorie Curry Harris

The truth behind those eyes.

Song Bird

Song bird song bird
Sing to me
Harmonize your sweet melody
From your perch upon the tree
Descend your solo flight unaccompanied
Sing your song of solidarity
Hear the desolation of a heart so heavy
For one song bird who sings alone
In the vastness of so many
Is in itself a metaphor
For human lives spent so lonely
How sad the song of a lone song bird
For God did not intend for us to be companionless
But instead to share our lives with others
To offer friendship and support
Guidance and advice
To marry and have families
To live our lives
The solo of a lone song bird
Is beautiful to hear
But when joined in a chorus
How powerful their voices become
When a single voice becomes more than one.

Lorie Curry Harris

Don't See Color See Soul

When upon my face
You cast your gaze
Is your first thought of my race
White, African American, Latino or Asian
Is it then that you pass your judgment
By the color of one's skin
Never looking passed their nationality
To find the person they are within
For no matter should there be given
To the color of one's skin
But instead look inside the soul
For we are all different
No person is the same
We just need to lend kindness
Friendship and politeness
For when God looks upon us
He never sees color
He only sees soul
So, let's lead by his example
Whether they be friend or foe
When looking upon another
Don't see color see soul.

Lorie Curry Harris

Love How Is It Defined

Is love defined by a gentle touch
A warm embrace
A tender kiss
Is love defined in kind words spoken
In respect given
Is love defined by home
Or nourishment of food taken
Is love defined by daily labors
Chores done check list completed
Is love defined by trust
Safety and security felt
Is love defined by the friendship made
Or the uniting of two lives
Love can be defined by all of these
But the greatest of love is defined
By giving of yourself
Completely to another
No judgements passed
Where each is seen as equals
Yes, true love is defined
By giving of it unconditionally.

Lorie Curry Harris

So Long

So long my friend
Who I have known through the year
I hope that you remember
The good times and the tears
But as this journey ends
I hope you understand
I will always remember you
And I certainly won't forget
Your smile or your face
And your humble grace
But until we meet again
So long my friend.

Lorie Curry Harris

Character

Character isn't something
We are born with or taught
It's simply found within yourself
As you travel down this journey of life
Character comes from the lessons
And trials we have faced
Character is found
In the way you conduct yourself
When facing adversity
Whether you are quick tempered
Or sharp with your tongue
Your character shows
What kind of person you are
Moral, vindictive
Gracious or kind
If asked by others
What your character is
How would you be described.

Lorie Curry Harris

Tranquility

You calm your mind
Lay down your head to rest
Be still in the quiet
Find some peacefulness
Let go your worries
Your fear and stress
Take a deep breath
Now exhale it out
Find your center
Be serene
In this moment while reposed
Learn the ability to be placid
And you will know
Tranquility in places
That are disturbed.

Lorie Curry Harris

Book One: Just Beyond The Sunrise

BOOK TWO

COLORS
OF CHARACTER
Revised Edition
By
LORIE CURRY HARRIS

PUBLISHED by PARABLES
Earthly Stories with a Heavenly Meaning

Lorie Curry Harris

Book Two: Colors Of Character

BOOK TWO

COLORS
OF CHARACTER
Revised Edition
BY
LORIE CURRY HARRIS

PUBLISHED by PARABLES
Earthly Stories with a Heavenly Meaning

Lorie Curry Harris

Book 1: Just Beyond The Sunset
Book 2: Colors Of Character
Lorie Curry Harris

Published By Parables
May, 2020

All Rights Reserved. No part of this book may be reproduced or utilized in any form or by any means, electronic or mechanical, including photocopying, recording, or by any information storage and retrieval system, without permission in writing from the author.

    Printed in the United States of America

Readers should be aware that Internet Web sites offered as citations and/or sources for further information may have been changed or disappeared between the time this was written and the time it is read.

Book Two: Colors Of Character

Table of Contents
The Weeping Willow
Butterfly Wings
Native Land
Least We Forget
Masquerade
Soar Again
Seasons
What Happened To Simplicity
Doubt
The Lost
Life Played In Music
Learn From Nature
Homeless Not Helpless
In Another
Believe
You Would Never Know Now
The Life She's Chosen
Love From Above
The Journey
Empty Womb
Morning
The Solider
Memories Of A Vet
Unsung Hero
A Father
Mother
My Brother

Father By Choice
A Daughter's Love
Daddy's Little Girl
Little One
A Giving Heart
His Trials
Borrowed Time
Grandmothers Hand
Baby Boy
Memory Lane
More Special Than She Knows
The Lord's Thoughts
Light
My Love
The Poet
At His Command
Eternity
What Does God See
Christmas Cheer
Peace Is Found
Anger
Bitterness
Mother You Were To Me

The Weeping Willow

Noticing the weeping willow
Standing tall upon the hill
Her long limbs bellowing
With the whispers of the wind
She bends and sways like music notes
Never breaking from the storms
Dancing along with natures song
There is sadness to her beauty
A sense of softness to her touch
You find comfort under her branches
Beneath her soft blanket of lullabies
Which gives me reason to ponder
Why does the weeping willow cry?
She cries for all mankind

Lorie Curry Harris

Butterfly Wings

Watching the butterfly climb a tree
Crawl across the branches
And begin to weave
High above the ground upon that limb
Carefully spins its cocoon of silk
Wrapping itself safe inside
Protected from the elements of life
The raging storms and bitter cold
It can not be tousled
From the winds that blow
For the caterpillar has a strong hold
Where it has fastened itself
For its journey home
Prepared for the long winters nap
Excitement can be felt
For the caterpillar knows
As it slumbers and waits
A miracle is taking place
The scars upon its flesh are healed
The ugliness of disappointment and fear
At last, begin to disappear
The transformation there begins
As healing of its soul descends
It's struggle upon the ground is no more
For a new creature is being formed
With the renewing of spring and regrowth
The warm sunrays
Awakens the caterpillar's heart

Emerging from its perch
Hiding high up in the tree
Is the most gorgeous butterfly
You had ever seen
With all the colors of the rainbow
In its butterfly wings
Watch it fly, fly across the sky
Bidding its old life goodbye
With the freedom
That could only be found
By the transformation
Of letting go of self
So fly, fly high
With all the colors of character
Upon your wings.

Native Land

They lived on the mountain side
And in the meadows green
Down in the valleys
Amongst the trees
Lived off the land
Fishing the streams
Killing the buffalo
For their meat
They waste not a scrap
Even using the hide
To make skillfully
Their clothes and tepees
Beautiful craftsman of the buffalo skin
So many talents there are in their tribe
With colorful necklace made from beads
And craftly painted pottery
Or the adornment of the feather head dress
Steadfast in culture and spiritual beliefs
Their heritage runs deep
Peaceful people that were misunderstood
So out of fear and ignorance
A decision was made
To take away all they knew to be
Forced from their native land
Where they lived for centuries
To be placed in a prison of reservation
What lively hood could there be found
Upon this plot of ground

They did not leave without a fight
Who would in their plight?
No fear was there to be
Of these people they seen
With tan colored skin
And long flowing hair
Gone silent are the beating drums
And no do the buffalo roam
No more to be found
Upon their native land
Is the meadow green
Or the fishing streams
It has all been killed
In the name of industry
There are lessons to be found
From the wrongs long ago
Do not judge
What you do not know

Least We Forget

See the man on the street
Speaking of God's saving grace
See the people with signs
Protesting against what they feel is wrong
See the voters at the poles
Putting into office friend or foe
Hear the music coming from cars
No matter the beat, it's your right to choose
Watching the talk shows on tv
Hearing the news from all different views
See the student standing there
In the library full
With books upon the shelves
See the business man
With newspaper in hand
Reading from the journalist pen
See the familics tucked safely in
You can lay your head down peacefully
For in America, we have freedom to choose
Freedom to vote and go to school
Freedom of speech and of beliefs
But we seem to forget at what cost is paid
For the liberties bestowed
For they fought for the red, white and blue
Sacrificing themselves for you
Least we forget the bravery of those
Who gave of themselves to uphold
The American values freedoms and rights

Lorie Curry Harris

So, when you lay your head down
On your pillow at night
Thank God for the military
Who decided to fight.

Masquerade

He lives behind his mask
They come in different forms
Some are smiling, full of laughs
Some are angry and full of strife
Some are sad and full of tears
He lives his life behind them all
Wondering each day which one will befall
What façade can he show today
That would hide whose locked away
The battle, the turmoil that rages within
Continues the drama of his play
His own expression becoming blank
From playing the masquerade
Of what others think he should be
One day he may find the bravery
To throw away the script
Step out from behind the curtain
And be the man he was meant to be.

Lorie Curry Harris

Soar Again

Silence the voices in my head
Chase away the darkness of my days
Lift my troubles with the sunrise rays
Dry my tears with the flutter
Of the butterfly's wings
Send me joy in the canaries' song
Let me find pleasure in the gentle breeze
Opening my senses
To what all I have longed and dreamed
Let hope renew like the babbling brook
Restoring to self all that life took
Like the phoenix bird finds rebirth
Rise up, and soar again.

Lorie Curry Harris

Season's

When tears fall down
Like springtime rain
And your dream are shattered on the windowpane
A cold wind blows deep in your soul
Carrying away your hopes and goals
Like leaves on an autumn day
You feel betrayed and bruised and stomped upon
Like the vine ripened grapes made for wine
Your lost in the shadows of your former self
No longer recognizing the reflection in the mirror
How do you find your way back
Through the storm
Like your footprints being lost in a snowy blizzard
Try to find your compass locked deep inside
Explore the adventures that it hides
Point yourself towards brighter tomorrows
Like sunbeams bursting through the clouds
And one day soon you will begin to hear
The beauty in the season's song
The cleansing in the springtime rain
The healing warmth of the summer rays
The laughter in the dancing autumn leaves
And yes, even in the bitterness of winter
There is hope to be found
Because life's circle all begins again
With the renewing of spring.

Lorie Curry Harris

Book Two: Colors Of Character

What Happened To Simplicity

In todays' day and age
It's all about high tech and speed
What happened to simplicity
Remember playing hide and seek
Tag, kick ball and red rover red rover
Now it's all video games and tv
Families use to sit around the dinner table
Talking about the happenings of their day
Joking and laughing together
Enjoying each other's company
Now it's fast food and drive thru
Emails and text messaging
Remember the fresh clean crisp scent
Of clothes being dried in the summer breeze
A hint of the outdoors in the clothes you wear
Or the excitement you felt waiting for nightfall
So you could catch fire flies in mason jars
Remember the fun you found
Pitching a tent and sleeping on the ground
The star lit sky above your head
Tree frogs singing, crickets chirping
The camp fire crackling and glowing
And marshmallows melting on the end of your stick
Now it's r.v.s and air conditioning
Technology is helpful I know
But I miss the days of not so long ago
Where we moved at a slower pace

Time was taken to say hello to neighbors
No back stabbing or corporate race
Families took time to say grace
You helped those in need without a thought
Now people say what's in it for me
They say technology is moving us forward
For a better future, better tomorrows'
But I say it's moving us away
From what's most important
Family values and a harmonious life
Maybe that's why we are always looking back
And talking about the good ole days
Where we could always find simplicity

Doubt

Doubt resides in the what if's
And could have been
The yester year of days long past
Playing out in your mind's eye
Your childhood plans
Your adolescent dreams
The fleeting moments of measuring yourself
Questioning the value of self-worth
And is also found in the presence of today
As you reach for all you have ever dreamed
You can hear it whispering there
As you nurture all that is good and fair
You will always find doubt lurking
In the shadows of a dream.

The Lost

Your child left one morning
With back pack in hand
Heading off to another school day
Leaving their room in complete disarray
You sit sipping your coffee and watching the news
Completely unaware of what this day would ensue
For you didn't know then what you would later be told
That your child has gone missing, with no trace or clues
Your whole world crashes in, your heart sinks to your toes
This isn't happening, this can't be true
There is some mistake, I am begging you
As days begin to run one into the other
Time has quickly turned to years
Your tears now silently flow
Their room is left the same as it was
How can you move forward when there is no way to know
What fate had befallen you child long ago
Now listed among the lost of so many
With question that may forever remain unanswered
So, you leave a candle brightly burning
Down deeply in your soul
Because it's the only way you can keep going
Living in hope, even if unknown.

Life Played In Music

Life is like a sheet of music
Every stanza sings a different tune
Every melody uniquely played
Harmoniously flowing together
In the realm of indifference
You can still find similarities
Whither it be the grace of ballet
Or the sincerity found in a serenade
Maybe for you the glee is found
With the soft cappella sound
Or in the romance of a ballad
No matter if this be your prelude piece
The time to sing duet
Or the chance to dance solo
Always remember to be the maestro of your own symphony.

Learn From Nature

See the redwood tree growing tall
No matter the adversities it still stands strong
Like cardinal birds, who mate for life
They weather the storms, no matter the fight
See the mallards floating there on the pond
Gracefully swimming, or so you would think
But underneath closely you see
They struggle to stay a float
The hummingbird so small and fragile
Approaches cautiously
But its beauty magnifies its wonder
What lessons we could learn from nature
Like the ocean waves bringing in the tide
I will forever be at your side.

Lorie Curry Harris

Homeless Not Helpless

No walls of four, no grass of green
No sheltered roof to sleep beneath
No fresh water from the tap
No place to take a bath
A cardboard box you now call home
An overpass to sleep beneath
A rainy day becomes your shower
Your tattered cloths barley keeps you warm
From the storms' that passing through
Your stomach grumbles from the hunger
And you again begin to wonder
Where will I find food today
What kind stranger will pass my way
Will they see past the image of
The shattered person of my former self
Will they look me in the eye
And find the hope that still resides
Will this forever be
My home upon the concrete
Will I just begin to fade
And become just part of the landscape
I hope not, I pray not
For in me there still leaves a dream
No pity do I seek
If people could just look and see
Deep inside still is the former me.

Lorie Curry Harris

In Another

Silent tears fall on her pillow
For the child she will never know
Nights pass slowly for her now
As she dreams of how her child grows
In another home, not her own
Her child is being loved and cared for
In another mothers' arms, not her own
Her child is being snuggled and cuddled
In another bed her child is tucked tightly in
As bedtime stories and good nights are said
In another her child finds comfort
In another her child feels loved
Another hears, I love you mommy
Another sees her child grow
Another gets to watch the stepping stones
And one day another will hear
The lovely sweet words of grandma
She hopes and prays and even dreams
That one day her child will understand
She was so young the day her baby was born
She had to give her child away
To give her child a chance
To give her child better
To give her child a life
What selfless gift she gave that day
The day she gave her heart away.

Lorie Curry Harris

Believe
Don't cast your stones
Into the wishing well
Nor wish upon a falling star
Don't believe in the myth
Of the magic it is told to behold
What power could there possibly be
In the water hole or a star burning out
Why do we have to look to other things
To wish upon and believe
We all possess within ourselves
An inner source of being
Where confidence and self-worth reside
We all have our own ability
To make true all that we dream
You only need look in the mirror
To find in what to believe.

Lorie Curry Harris

You Would Never Know Now

You would never know now
The nightmare that was her past
The horrors and fright
The pain and strife
You would never know now
By the smile that she wears
That she cried herself to sleep each night
You would never know now
By the light in her eyes
That once all you could find was despair
You would never know now
By the confidence she holds
That once she was completely beaten down
You would never know now
From the way she has found her voice
That once she was silenced by fear
You would never know now
From the freedom she feels
She was once imprisoned by another's anger
You would never know now
Because she walked away
Found her courage and inner strength
Learned not only how to love
But also, to love herself
No, you would never know now.

Lorie Curry Harris

The Life She's Chosen

Like winter creeps across the land
Coldness blows deep in her soul
Life has cast her out like a jezebel
Her anger builds like a forest fire
Raging deep within
Devouring anything that gets to close
She's built a wall like a fortress around herself
No way to chip the mortar she's set-in place
Each brick was placed painstakingly
Giving each its own name
Some people think she likes the bricks she's made
They say its an excuse to keep people away
It's most possible that there right
But what reason do they have to judge her life
They have not walked her path
Or felt her tears
How sad she really is
From having wasted all these years
But she doesn't know how to let go
Her pain has become her comfort
Her anger is her defense
Her disappointments, her life's definition
But somewhere it all has to stop
The light has to come back in
She has to learn to let go
So, let the calming ocean waves
Settle all her fears
Let springtime rain extinguish the fire

That's raging within
Let summer winds knock down her walls
And allow love back in
Let time erase the memories
Of the names upon the bricks
Let the wagging tongues of others
Finally begin to cease
For she stands in judgement of God alone
For the life she's chosen to lead.

Love From Above

The fog moves across the land
Like a heavy cloak
Mysterious and white
Against the dark of night
How mystifying it seems to be
Simply appearing for you to see
Though you cannot touch it with your hand
It simply moves right through
And just as quickly as it came
It vanishes from view
Leaving a dampness in the air
Letting you know it was there
Sometimes angles come this way
Touch your life on a difficult day
There briefly, with the softest touch
To convey to you the love from above.

Lorie Curry Harris

The Journey

As I travel down this road
This journey we call life
I can't help but to look back
On the childhood of my past
The innocence of a young girl stolen
By an abuser in the night
The bumps, the bruises the detours set in place
How does a child overcome the obstacles'
Of such overwhelming disarray
Only by God's amazing grace
Do I find my inner strength within
As he turns the bad to good
And he molds me
Into the woman I am today
The heart of a survivor
Now beats in my chest
The past will always plaque me
Of that there is no doubt
But it is now just a memory
No more does it define me
Tomorrow is on the horizon
The future is looking bright
The darkness has moved into the shadows
Emerging, is God's saving light.

Lorie Curry Harris

Empty Womb

No sweet lullabies, no babies' cries
No late feedings in the night
No pitter patter of tiny feet
No swaddling bundle fast asleep
No terrible twos to get through
No sleepy whispers of I love you
No growing pains to overcome
No bitter sweet farewells
No tiny heart beat sounds
Will there ever be found
Inside this woman fare
For God in his wisdom
Had only given
The sound of empty womb.

Lorie Curry Harris

Morning

See the early morning sky
Bursting into a colorful orange hue
Hear the birds singing
Good morning to you
Feel the gentle kiss
Of the morning dew
Smell the beautiful aroma
Of the flowers opening their blooms
Feel the slight breeze
Tickling your hair
This is God, letting us know he's there.

Lorie Curry Harris

The Soldier

No words can convey the gratitude
Of an American civilian today
For all the sacrifices the soldier has made
For bearing arms on battlefields
On foreign soil or ocean seas
Across the sky and to desert land
Where God has held your hand
What fears you must have felt
Where on the battlefield your foot first stepped
What horrors you must have seen
When friends you made fell at your feet
How weary it must all have been
When at long last your task at end
Only to know tomorrow holds
Uncertainty of what's unknown
But you continue to press on
Oh, how brave the soldier's heart
As you maintain in our plight
To stand where we don't have to fight.

Lorie Curry Harris

Memories Of A Vet

Although your body does not lay
In a battlefield unmarked grave
You may not bare wounds upon your flesh
No outward signs of distress
Your scars lay deeper locked inside
Only to be found upon your soul and mind
Now safely home there's things you miss
A restful night's sleep, peaceful bliss
This all evades you in the night sky
As those memories play out in your tired eyes
You now find pleasure in the simple things
A child's laugh or a bird when it sings
Your footsteps lay heavy with the weight of the past
Though others see hero
You don't see that within yourself
Decorated with medals, no matter to you
You just did your job, you seen it through
Army, Air Force, Navy, Marine
You all carry with you these memories
One day they will lay a flag
Upon your chest
To be peacefully laid to rest
Only then does your war truly end.

Lorie Curry Harris

Unsung Hero

My days just ran one into the other
As the wounded continuously filed in
The agony was written upon each face
Their bodies were torn, flesh ripped apart
Remnants of shrapnel embedded in their skin
Their screams could be heard in my dreams each night
If I could ever dream at all again
These fallen men and women needing my aid
Their lives have been changed in an instant
They will never be the same
I will never be the same
They grab your hand and beg for you
Please oh please just make it stop
Make the pain go away
I try to aid, I try to comfort
I cry oh God please, make the fighting stop
Silence the guns end the madness
Then I hear,
Nurse, more wounded coming in.

Lorie Curry Harris

A Father

A father teaches his children to grow
He passes on his personality and traits
He gives to them courage and grace
He teaches them about love and faith
Not only in words but by example
A father's discipline is firm
But his heart gentle
As a child you remember
What a giant he seemed to be
But with your little hand in his
You could do anything
He went from teaching you how to ride a bike, to how to drive a car
He listened when you talked
And held you when you cried
A father gives you away on your wedding day
Or stands beside you as your best man
And as you see your father be a grandfather
Your reminded of your childhood
When he bounced you on his knee and made you laugh
A father is so many things you see
He's a teacher, a disciplinarian, a play mate and a best friend
But most of all he's your hero
That's the kind of father I think you to be.

Lorie Curry Harris

Mother

She was so young when her little ones came along
You would never know by looking
The struggles that she faced
The smiling eyes she shown to her children
Hid the fact they never knew
Her heart was broken in a million pieces
By the empty promises that never came true
She found herself alone
Aside from her little ones
She gave them all she knew to give
No matter what the cost
She picked herself up each morning
Starting another day anew
She found a way to make it work
She found a way to heal the hurt
Her children were her refuge
The safe harbor from the storm
Her guiding light, was their laughter
Her call to home was their hugs
Her anchor was their love
She could not see then
The example that she set
For as she struggled, she shown them
As she fought, she shown them
As she healed, she shown them
As she was their mother, she shown them
She had taught them how to live.

Lorie Curry Harris

My Brother

As children we had the innocence of being young
Spending our days in laughter and fun
Dreaming about a future of happiness and love
And as the years went by and we grew older
We learned to appreciate the values of others
And in doing so I found a sibling bound
That is unbreakable through time or death
You taught me so much in your time here
You were an ear who listened in time of trouble
A shoulder to lean on when things went wrong
A hand to cling to when you needed to be rescued
A hug to help your pain and calm your fears
A smile to make you laugh and forget your worries
A tender heart who cared for all who knew you
So how do I say goodbye
How do I let you go?
You were my confidant, my best friend
You will live forever in my heart
Goodbye, goodbye my brother.

Lorie Curry Harris

Father By Choice

I was just a little girl
When you entered our lives
The day we became a family of five
Adjustments had to be made
No question of that
But you never pushed
You just sat quietly back
Patiently waiting perhaps already knowing
The bond that time and love would be forming
For there was no way for us to know then
The love in your heart that was already growing
For the children of this family
You were joining
Though a man of few words
Rarely speaking of feelings
You showed us each day
The secret your heart was keeping
That you loved us by choice
You were our father by choice
Though we were not bound by blood
We would forever be bound by love.

Lorie Curry Harris

A Daughter's Love

She does not leave her care alone
To the nursing staff of the home
She's there each day to see she's fed
And be gently put to bed
Such love is found upon her face
With each kind word
Every warm embrace
A smile you will always see
For she is still making precious memories
What tenderness she bestows
She treats her with dignity and grace
Some fear is found behind her eyes
As roles are reversed, she now finds
Herself being the mother
Instead of the daughter
Her frailty you cannot hide
Her memory not as sharp
But as her eyes finds her daughter
A light passes upon her face
For she knows
She is always wrapped
In her daughter's love.

Lorie Curry Harris

Daddy's Little Girl

I'm sure, if I stepped into your shoes
For just a moment I would see
Though the years have slipped by
You still see, daddy's little girl
With thin blonde hair
And bright blue eyes
And you search her eyes and see
If daddy's little girl is still there
Because years were stolen
Away from us,
Time has sort of stood still
And now standing before you
In place of daddy's little girl
Is a grown woman
Gone are the pig tails and dolls
The little shoes and toys
It's as if we were thrown forward in time
We will never have the memories
We wish we could have
Of summer days and growing up
Of broken hearts and growing pains
Or giving me away on my wedding day
But we can't turn back time
And live on what if's
So, let's make memories now
Of summer days and growing older

Lorie Curry Harris

And be thankful
We were brought back together,
In this lifetime
No matter how old a daughter gets
She will always be, daddy's little girl.

Little One

You were conceived in love my little one
A gift from above
Our bond began to form
Before you were even born
I cherished our moments just you and me
Our mommy time you see
You started to grow in the womb
Your fingers and toes your head and nose
Oh, how you moved and kicked about
Feeling your movements from without
I readied your room in preparation
With blankets, clothes and toys
Awaiting your arrival with anticipation
When finally, your birthday came
And they placed you on my chest
It was astonishing to, at long last see
Your precious little face
My heart was overflowing with joy
Our family circle now complete
Mother such a simple word
That holds so much meaning
Mother hood such a wonderous thing.

Lorie Curry Harris

A Giving Heart

A gentle soul, this man I know
With giving smiling eyes
Although he has seen
A nightmare of things
It waivers not his heart
He gives to all of those he knows
No repayment does he seek
Just simple gratitude's and thank you
Is all he ever needs
For a family man is he
A doting father that's plain to see
Devoted to his wife
With such a giving heart.

Lorie Curry Harris

His Trials

He has fought so many battles in his life
Some in war and some in strife
The mountaintops he has seen are few
But his valleys have been many
How broad his shoulders
Must have to be, to carry the weight
Of such catastrophe
It seems each time the ends in sight
There's another obstacle he must fight
How much more must he take
How much more must he face
His faith begins to waiver
As he looks to the sky, he asks why
He is an honest man
He lives his life in the word
Why must he continue to feel
That his life has to be a daily struggle
For those of us who know him well
He will pick himself up
He will brush himself off
He will begin another day anew
For the love for his family is strong
And they will see him through.

Lorie Curry Harris

Borrowed Time

The news came today
That you had passed away
The lord called you home
In heaven you now stay
No more struggle, no more pain
Your fight is done, your race is run
It's bitter sweet for those you leave
We will miss our uncle,
Our father, our brother
Our borrowed time has now ended
We are grateful for the extra years
To share a laugh, a hug a tear
So, rest now for we know
Your souls at peace, your hearts at ease.

Lorie Curry Harris

Grandmothers Hand

The funeral is over
And the flowers are dead
But her memory still lingers in my head
I still remember her soft gentle hand
Now she walks in the promise land
I will keep her alive
In my heart and my mind
But it's time to let go
Of Grandmothers hand.

Lorie Curry Harris

Baby Boy

I was there the day you were born
On early April morn
Everyone was waiting
For that wonderful bundle of joy
But your heart wasn't quite right
And that's were you began your fight
As you struggled each day for your life
I watched you with love and admiration
When inside I was feeling
Anger and frustration
So, I prayed to God
To heal you from your pain
He took you to heaven
And there you would gain
Health and sweet peace
In his arms you would lay
In rest and comfort
Which leads me to say
We love you,
And we are awaiting the day
When we see you in heaven
On that glorious reunion day.

Lorie Curry Harris

Memory Lane

I took a stroll down memory lane
And my thoughts recollected
Of a man whose eyes had signs of pain
From past heartache and broken dreams
But also, if you looked you could also see
A sparkle of hope
For a love that might be
For the eyes are a window to the heart
And I could see
A love shinning inside of him
That was just waiting to be released
And as his eyes met a young lady's
That love was set free
And as he reached to grasp her hand
She looked in his eyes and she seen
The man of her dreams
They rejoiced in their summer love
And planned a future
To share their lives as one
But the young lady let the man go
Hurting herself and him also
Which brings us back
To the reality of today, those memories
She will keep close to her heart
Memory lane reminds me
I let my one true love slip away.

Lorie Curry Harris

More Special Than She Knows

She's stylish and chic, spunky and fun
Underneath it all, she's a heart full of love
Her beauty radiates from the inside out
She doesn't see herself
As those who love her do
A selfless person, always giving to others
A friend you can count on
When the chips are down
A mother devoted to her child
She's always trying to please
No matter the cost
Putting others needs above her own
Hardly ever using the word no
She's like a burst of sunshine
On a cloudy day
Or a flower blooming in the snow
One thing is for certain
No doubt of that
Your life is richer, better
Just for having known her.

Lorie Curry Harris

The Lord's Thoughts

I imagine with the way things are today
That the Lord is wondering
What has happened to my children
Whatever happened to
The happiness and joy
Why are my people turning
To the wickedness of this world
Instead of believing
In the promises in my word
Have I not taught you to have faith in me
And I will supply you with
Whatever your need may be
I know you've had trouble
And more valley's than mountain tops
But if you would only
Look beside you and see
I was always standing with you
Even when you left me.

Lorie Curry Harris

Light

You know the time of day
When the sun sets and darkness falls
So slowly you don't notice it at all
It is at this moment a hush settles in
As light goes away and darkness begins
The stars come out like eyes from heaven
As silence grows stronger
And darkness deeper
You look to the sky and wonder
Where is he
Because you feel alone
In your vastness of trouble
Like the light being taken
By the darkness of night
The sun shines brightly in the day
And no one notices to see
But what is oft forgotten
Is the light shines brightest
In the darkness
Shinning his light
To show us his pathway.

Lorie Curry Harris

My Love

This person I see before me
The man and love of my life
He sees to every need I have
Making sure I want for nothing
He treats me with such tenderness
He treats me with such respect
He sees right to the soul of me
His love has given me the ability
To see in myself what others see
To believe that I could do anything
To know with all certainty
No matter what obstacles
No matter what trials or twist or turns
That our lives together we must face
He will always stand with me
His love will never waiver
His faith in me will never falter
Our love will never wither
In his arms you find serenity
In his embrace you find security
In his kiss you find the passion
In his eyes you find our story
Of our two hearts, of our two lives
Destine to find each other
Destine to be together
Already withstanding the test of time
Already knowing that with each other

Lorie Curry Harris

We have found peace
We have found true joy
We have found home.

The Poet

She is quiet and shy, reserved and unsure
She had to find an outlet
Someway to show
All the feelings and thoughts
She had inside her soul
So, she sat down with pen and paper
The words just pouring out
This form of expression freeing her
To tell the secrets that she holds
As the words washed over the paper
There was a cleansing deep inside
For each sentenced formed
She had found the answer
The healing of her mind.

At His Command

God knows I try
I've been hurt so many times
Sometimes I don't understand
But my life is in his hands
And with him, I will take my stand
To face the world, at his command.

Lorie Curry Harris

Eternity

Oh Father help me please
Lead me wherever you need me be
Let your will be done through me
Let others see my life shine towards thee
So they will long
For your love and purity
Let my life be a testimony for thee
Because through it all
Oh, Lord let them see
You're the one
Who holds the key to eternity.

Lorie Curry Harris

Book Two: Colors Of Character

What Does God See

A woman beaten and abused
Left upon the streets
With tears flowing down her cheeks
People pass her by and maybe think
She has gotten what she deserves
This woman of the streets
But what does God see
A man begging, standing with a sign
In tattered clothes and
Whiskey on his breath, begging for food
People pass him by and maybe think
Worthless drunk
But what does God see
A teenage girl in front of an abortion clinic
Feeling tossed aside like garbage and used
People pass her by and maybe think
How dare you take the life of that child
But what does God see
Watching a murder trial on tv
People watching maybe think
That criminal doesn't deserve to live
But what does God see
As a society we are quick to judge
Never looking closely at one's soul
No thought ever crossing our minds
As of why that person is where they are
Why the decision they are making

Came to be
But what does God see
When seeing the woman of the streets
God sends her mercy and saving grace
Washing away the sins of before
Opening her heart to so much more
When seeing the drunk with his sign
God sends healing of his heart and mind
Washing away the demons of his past
Allowing light in his soul once again
When seeing the teenage girl at the clinic
God's heart begins to break
For two lives have forever been changed
For only he should take a life
God wraps his arms around her strongly
Allowing her to lean on him
For in his arms
Your sheltered from the storms
In his embrace peace is found
By his forgiveness
You are once whole again
In his love you learn to forgive
Not only others but yourself
What a wonderful world this would be
If we would stop sitting
In judgement of others
And see what God sees.

Christmas Cheer

Its that wonderful time of year
With Christmas time drawing near
When everyone is filled
With holiday cheer
Where the troubles that plague you
Are forgotten for awhile
As the joy of the season
Sinks into your heart
A new year approaching
With new fulfillments to find
Hope renewing with abundance divine
The Christmas tree adorned
With ornaments and lights
The laughter filling the house each night
The snow covering the ground
In a blanket of white
Sleigh bells jingling
Making the most beautiful sound
Carolers singing being heard all around
Families reunited on this Christmas day
To celebrate the season of Jesus birthday
As you open your presents under the tree
Never forget the reason
This day came to be
So, lets gather our hands
Together in prayer
Lift our voices of thanks
Up to God to hear.

Lorie Curry Harris

Peace Is Found

While walking down the wooded trail
Gazing at natures beauty
Birds are singing all around
Animals scurrying on the ground
A soft wind blows swaying the trees
Back and forth in the breeze
And in this moment peace is found
As you travel further down the trail
A stream is running there
Listen closely to its sound
For in this moment peace is found
As it washes over your soul to cleanse
Now you find yourself in a valley deep
Be still and listen closely to hear
For God is standing very near
As your knees hit the ground
In this moment peace is found
For God has brought you through
Your trials of life
You look up towards the sky
And you see the mountain standing high
Steadfast and strong in its majestic beauty
And in this moment peace is found
For in your heart, you know
No matter the trail you take
No matter the valley deep
You will always soar up on eagles' wings
To the mountain top to see

Gods' beauty all around
The cleansing of the water streams
The forgiveness in the breeze
The joy as the bird sings
And in the freeing
Of your heart to know
In God, peace will always be found.

Anger

Don't let anger enrage your thoughts
Become irritated and cross
Don't let anger infuriate your heart
Becoming full of fury and wrath
Don't let anger take over your life
Move into your soul and reside
Taking over your mind
Finding displeasure all around
Becoming annoyed at every little thing
Letting everyone feel your outrage
Where your words come fuming
Out your mouth
Don't let anger kill your soul
And push away all the good you know
Don't let anger fester under your skin
Causing your blood to boil
Then your face turns red
And your heart to become cold
Instead, learn to let go
Find the pleasure in the simple things
Think before a word is said
Then breath, and count to ten.

Lorie Curry Harris

Bitterness

Bitterness can grow
From the smallest seed
Transplant itself in your soul to feed
Off all the disappointments,
Anger and strife
You have been through in your life
Bitterness can turn your heart to stone
And you will find yourself all alone
Bitterness devours from the inside out
Destroying the person you are supposed to be at about
It takes away all your wants and needs
Your happiness your joy
Your inner being
Till at last all that is found
Is just an empty shell of yourself
No more ambitions or dreams to fulfill
No more goals to achieve
No life to lead
For when you allow bitterness to grow
Not even hope, is renewing.

Lorie Curry Harris

Mother You Were To Me

Every time I stumbled
Scraped a knee or cried
You were always at my side
When growing up, I looked to you
To show to me the person I should be
What I found was humbling
For in you I could always find
A heart that was gentle and kind
No judgement did you pass upon me
For mistakes or decisions made hastily
You just simply offered
Your warm embrace
For whatever I may face
No matter the way I viewed myself
You were there to encourage
And lift me up high
To see myself through your eyes
The sacrifices you made for me
Did not go unnoticed
Oh, don't you see
Now that I'm grown
I hope only to be
At least half the mother you were to me.

Lorie Curry Harris

May you find in this collection of poems, appreciation and sacrifices made by others. Find your faith renewed, and yourself restored. Your adversities may seem greater than yourself and your mistakes may forever plague you. Forgive yourself as God has forgiven you. Believe in yourself and second chances. May you be uplifted from heartache and loss. Some of these poems were written from my own life experiences so I understand. Have faith in Gods unconditional love. Appreciate the simplest things and all the colors of character around you, and know there is always hope, just beyond the sunrise. Revised editions of, Colors of Character and Just Beyond the Sunrise are included together.

I reside in Kentucky, where I was born and raised. I started writing at the age of 11. Finding a sense of freedom in this form of expression. Losing myself in the rhythm of rhyme. Healing to the soul peace to the mind. I have been married since 2010. I look at my poems as artwork, if you will. Little short stories painted in words of rhyme.

www.ingramcontent.com/pod-product-compliance
Lightning Source LLC
Chambersburg PA
CBHW021424070526
44577CB00001B/53